Dare to be a Mighty Warrior Prayer Journal

By Mikaela Vincent

Jesus is calling you to a life of power, purpose, and freedom.

Stand up and fight.

Step into the adventure...

Mikaela Vincent
More Than A Conqueror Books

We're not just about books. We're about books that make a difference in the lives of those you care about.

MoreThanAConquerorBooks.com

Follow Mikaela Vincent:

Facebook Page: **Mikaela.Vincent.author**

Facebook Profile: **Mikaela.Vincent.MoreThanAConquerorBooks**

Instagram: **Mikaela.Vincent**

Twitter: **Mikaela_Vincent**

Pinterest: **Mikaela Vincent: More Than A Conqueror Books**

Blog: **www.MoreThanAConquerorBooks.wordpress.com**

Although this prayer journal can be used on its own,
it was created to accompany

Dare to Be a Mighty Warrior
by Mikaela Vincent

Practical, tactical, tried-and-true, effective spiritual warfare strategies for
today's husband, father, single man of God. Find freedom from strongholds, protect the ones you love, listen to God's voice, live in His power,
and win victory over darkness in the battlefield of the mind.
Fight evil and win. For real!

www.MoreThanAConquerorBooks.com

*(All proceeds the author receives go to sharing the Light in dark areas of
the world where few have heard of Christ.)*

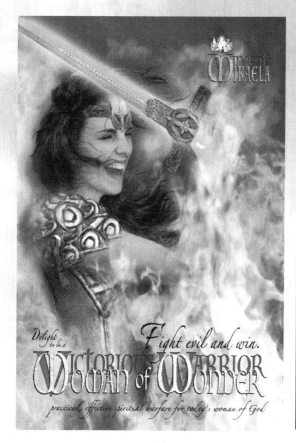

To my Godly father,
who taught me the power of prayer and
forgiveness ...

Thank you for following God's call to
the ends of the earth, and raising me
there under His covering and yours.
Thank you for modeling daily the
power of obedience to Christ, as you
sacrificially loved every single person you
met or even heard about. But to you, it
was no sacrifice at all. And that, my
dear Daddy, is how you handed me the
greatest weapon of all.

I am who I am today in Christ because
He loved me first through you.

"The Lord is with you, MIGHTY WARRIOR."

Judges 6:12b

"I pray that the eyes of your heart may be enlightened in order that you may know the hope to which He has called you, the riches of His glorious inheritance in His holy people, and **His incomparably great POWER for us who believe.** That POWER is the same as the **MIGHTY strength** He exerted when He raised Christ from the dead and seated Him at His right hand in the Heavenly realms." Ephesians 1:18-20

"The Lord is with me like a **MIGHTY WARRIOR**; so my persecutors will stumble and not prevail. They will fail and be thoroughly disgraced." Jeremiah 20:11

"The Lord will march out like a **CHAMPION**, like a **WARRIOR** He will stir up his zeal; **with a shout He will raise the battle cry and will triumph over His enemies.**" Isaiah 42:13

"Do not be afraid; do not be discouraged. **Be strong and courageous.** This is what the Lord will do to all the enemies you are going to fight." Joshua 10:25

My SON, I know life hasn't been easy for you. And you will yet encounter all the more evil in this world. But stand strong, steadfast in My love, firm in My divine purposes that are working out good in every situation. I am with you. And I am for you. Stand on Love and you will stand. 1 Corinthians 13:8-13, Romans 8:28.

Be still. Stop your striving. Settle your heart and mind. I am working a good thing in you, but you must rest in Me first before I will complete it. Trust Me. I know what I'm doing. Isaiah 30:15.

Lord, what blocks me from deeper oneness with You? Am I doubting You in some way? Are there sin habits or negative thought processes You want to set me free from? Are there any areas of my life I haven't given You yet? Show me.

(A comprehensive checklist for discovering sin habits and wrong thought processes that block us from oneness with Christ is available in the accompanying handbook of 100 practical spiritual warfare strategies for overcoming the enemy, *Dare to Be a Mighty Warrior*, by Mikaela Vincent, at www.MoreThanAConquerorBooks.com.)

My SON, why do you struggle so? I know you want to make a difference, to accomplish something of worth, to be appreciated, acknowledged.

Rest in Me. Don't let how others respond to you affect how you see yourself.

This battle was never meant to be about people liking you, agreeing with you, or doing what you think is best.

I called you to My purposes, not because I want others to think how great you are, but because *I* am the Great One Who draws all people to Myself.

I chose you to know Me, and to do great things together with Me in My empowering. But if you are too busy focusing on what others think of you, you will miss the joy of My presence and the power of My great love within you.

THIS BATTLE is for your own heart and mind, for oneness with Me. Are you ready to fight for that? I AM.

Know who you are in Me:

John 15:15: *Jesus, I am Your friend*

1 Corinthians 3:9: _____

1 Corinthians 6:19: _____

1 Corinthians 12:27: _____

2 Corinthians 5:20: _____

Hebrews 10:14: _____

Galatians 5:13: _____

Psalm 103:12: _____

Ephesians 2:10: _____

Acts 1:8: _____

Matthew 5:14: _____

Ephesians 2:19: _____

More:

You have an enemy, but it is not your brother or sister. This fight is not for comfort, selfish gain, to win an argument, get your way, prove a point, get ahead, have someone treat you the way you feel you should be treated, or anything else of this world.

Your enemy is the father of lies, Satan, and he is working night and day to drag you away from Me, the One Whose name is Truth.

Stand firm, My son, and do not waver. Know Who your King is, and love Me with all your heart. Fight for Kingdom matters, and you will find Me fighting by your side. 2 Corinthians 10:3-5, Ephesians 6:12.

Whatever you face in this world, I have already overcome
it. So, walk as one with Me, and we'll defeat it together.
John 5:19, 14:15.

You are My child, and in a
sense, you're still learning to
"walk" in some areas of your
life. If you fall, let Me pick
you up, show you what went
wrong, heal your wounds,
and empower you to run.
Hebrews 12:1-3.

But if ever you feel
condemnation, *it's not from
Me*. Romans 8:1. When I
convict you of sin, it is with
kindness to draw you
to Myself and heal you.
Romans 2:4.

Don't get distracted. You're busy with many things, but only one thing have I
asked of you: LOVE. Matthew 22:37-40.

Love is the key to victory in battle. Romans 8:35-39.

When you stand in Love, Satan loses. Every time. Love is the greatest Power.
For I AM LOVE. 1 John 4:7-21

You are in training for reigning, son of the Most High. That's why your trials feel so hard. But take heart. One day, when you're with Me in glory, there will be no more tears, problems, sins, or troubles for Me to rescue you from.

But right here, right now, this is your chance to know Me in all the mighty ways I am your Savior, Rescuer, Healer, Comforter, Strength.... Don't waste this time. Rest in Me. Let Me carry you through until you see Me face to face.

Stop dancing to the tune of what everyone thinks you should say, do, and be. You'll wear yourself out, and your joy will drain away. But My yoke is easy and My burden is light. Besides, I'm the only One Who knows where we're going. So, follow My lead and I'll take you there. Together.

Sometimes when you think you can't hear Me, it's because you're expecting Me to answer in a certain way. Psalm 29. Let Me speak to you in many exciting ways, and give you the perfect answer, whether it's the one you expected or not. Let Me be God.

I speak in many ways. Here are just a few I mention in My Word:

- The Word (2 Timothy 3:16-17)
- Circumstances (2 Corinthians 12:7-10; Psalm 40:1-3)
- Others (1 Corinthians 2:4-13)
- My still small voice in your mind and heart (Psalm 42:8)
- Dreams and visions (Acts 2:17)
- Impressions or urgings (Acts 15:28)
- A sense of peace (Philippians 4:7)
- Signs and wonders (Acts 2:17-21)
- Nature (Psalm 125; 19:1-4)

Sometimes, you can't hear what I'm saying because it's not what you're wanting to hear. Ask Me that question again, only this time, hand Me your desires and expectations. Let Me surprise you. Proverbs 3:5-7.

When I speak, you'll know it's Me, because
1. What I tell you will agree with My Word—all of it, not just a tiny portion. John 1:1.
2. My words line up with My character —especially My love. 1 John 4:7-16.
3. Whatever I say will draw you (and others around you) closer to Me. Galatians 5:22-25.

Filter your thoughts and what others say to you through this Three-Fold Sieve to discern the difference between truth and lies. 2 Corinthians 10:3-5.

What lies have others told me that I have believed?

_____
_____
_____
_____

What doubts, traditions or doctrines do I hold strongly to that do not agree with all of Your Word or with Your character of love and grace?

_____
_____
_____
_____
_____

How have my actions based on those beliefs hindered me from drawing closer to You and being used by You to draw others closer?

_____
_____
_____
_____
_____

What do You say to that, Lord? What is Your truth You want me to stand on and walk out in?

_____
_____
_____
_____
_____
_____

If you're not sure you're hearing Me right, or even at all, just keep handing Me your thoughts, asking Me questions, and looking for My answers. I may bring circumstances into your path you need to walk through to understand what I'm saying. Or I may be waiting until you surrender, or for just the right moment before I answer. So, don't worry if you can't "hear" Me right away. Just keep surrendering your heart to Me. Seek Me and you will find Me, if you look for Me in earnest. Jeremiah 29:12-13.

If you're finding it difficult to hear My voice, ask Me if any doubt lies are blocking you, like, "God speaks to others but not to me," or, "God only speaks in the Bible." Let Me unclog the ears of your heart. John 8:42-47, 10:27.

Lord, what lies am I believing about You or my ability to hear You that block me from listening?

_____

_____

_____

_____

When did I first start thinking that way? Why?

_____

_____

_____

_____

_____

What do You say about that, Lord? Please show me Your truth. Give me scripture to back up what You say, and set me free from my unbelief.

_____

_____

_____

_____

_____

_____

_____

_____

_____

_____

_____

_____

A lie is anything contrary to what I say. For example, believing you can't do anything right is a lie because of Philippians 4:13. Believing you're don't measure up is a lie because of Hebrews 10:14. Believing no one will love you if they know what you've done is a lie because of 1 Peter 4:8. What lies are you believing that oppose what I say? Those are the places where the enemy wants to keep you captive. Ask Me for My truth so I can set you free. John 8:32, 42-47.

Lies:	Truth:

Lord, is there anything You're saying to me that has felt like a lie? I want to believe You. Help my unbelief.

What do You say to that, Lord? What is Your truth?

The best way to recognize when the enemy is throwing you a lie is to walk so closely to Truth that any step outside the movement of My Spirit feels so wrong, you immediately click back in step. John 8:31-32, 42-47, 14:6, 15-17; Galatians 5:25.

Don't let your thoughts control you, My son. Hand them to Me.

Resist the enemy, and he will flee from you. James 4:7
Pursue Me, and you will find Me right here with you.

Do certain reactions seem to control you rather than My Spirit? Do you repent of a sin, and then turn around and do, say, or think that again, even though you don't want to? Romans 7:14-25. That is the picture of a spiritual stronghold — a wrong thought process, lie or sin habit that has a strong hold on you. Don't excuse it with, "That's just the way I am," or "That's just the way God made me." No! I didn't make you for sin. I made you for freedom! Let Me set you free. James 1:13, Galatians 5:1.

Love defies every enemy scheme. For I am Love. And when you receive My love and love others through My love, you are fighting on the winning side. 1 John 4:4-21.

You can use Galatians 5:22-23 as a heart gauge to find lies and wrong thought patterns you believe and act out of. Whenever you think or feel something negative outside the fruit of the Spirit, get alone with Me as soon as you can and ask Me where that comes from. When was the first time that feeling or attitude entered your heart? Let Me take you anywhere I want to take you and show you anything I want to show you. You need to see the lies you believe, so I can set you free with My truth.

Galatians 5:22-23.

The fruit of the Spirit:

_____

_____

_____

_____

_____

_____

_____

Are you feeling angry? Rejected? Discouraged? Afraid? Upset? Hurt? Betrayed? What thoughts make you feel that way?

What you feel is directly related to what you believe.

Lord, what have I felt or thought recently outside of the fruit of Your Spirit?

_____
_____
_____
_____
_____
_____
_____

Where did those thoughts come from? When did that reaction first enter my life?

_____
_____
_____
_____
_____
_____
_____

Help me feel what I felt when that happened. Show me the lies I believe.

_____
_____
_____
_____
_____
_____

Lord, You were there when that happened. What were You doing or saying? What do You say to my lies? What is Your truth?

_____
_____
_____
_____
_____
_____
_____

A lie is anything contrary to what I say, Who I am, and who you are in Me.

Lies are pressed into your heart through negative experiences, and become the building blocks for strongholds like pride, anger, lust, rejection, anxiety.

Strongholds are sins or wrong thought processes that have a strong hold on you — arguments that set themselves up against the knowledge of Me.

2 Corinthians 10:3-5

A stronghold controls your actions and reactions through the lies you believe, so that you react contrary to My Spirit, rather than in step with Me.

Your will isn't strong enough to break free. You need Someone stronger.

Most strongholds feel so "normal" you don't realize they're there. You might think, "Everyone struggles with that," or "That's just the way men think." That's because the enemy likes to hide your stronghold from you with guardian lies and whitewash.

Lord, what strongholds do I have that I didn't notice before?

What lies have been guarding them?

Lord, I don't want to think that way anymore. Tear down every lie and every stronghold with Your truth. Set me free....

I'm inviting you into freedom from negative thought processes through a deep encounter with Me, for I alone am Truth. Come and meet with Me. Let Me set you free from the reactions that cause you and others pain:

1. Whenever you feel something outside the fruit of My Spirit in Galatians 5:22-23, excuse yourself from the situation as soon as you can and come get alone with Me.

2. Ask Me where that attitude or feeling came from. Let Me take you anywhere I want to take you and show you anything I want to show you, even if it's a memory from long ago.

3. Whatever I bring to your mind, allow yourself to feel what you felt when that happened.

4. Ask Me to show you the lies you received (like, "No one will love me after what I've done," or "I'm not good enough," or "I have to stand up for my rights, because no one else will," etc.).

5. Ask Me for My truth. I was there when that happened. Ask Me what I was doing and saying.

6. Listen for My voice and look around for Me in your memory. Let Me renew your mind with My truth. Romans 12:1. I might remind you of a verse, or show you where I was and what I was saying and doing when that happened. Because I was there. You were just too distracted by what was happening to notice Me. Let Me heal your memory.

Lord, what negative reactions have risen up within me recently outside the fruit of Your Spirit?

_____

_____

_____

_____

_____

_____

Where did that reaction come from? When did I first react that way? Take me anywhere You want to take me and show me anything You want to show me.

_____

_____

_____

_____

_____

_____

_____

_____

When that happened, I felt ...

I thought ...

Lord, what do You say to that? What is Your truth to topple those lies? What were You saying and doing when that happened?

Lies have a wrong focus, like looking at your own unworthiness or inability rather than My greatness and power.

When I call you, it's not because of your ability or worthiness, but because of My worthiness and My love for you. In fact, I will often call you to do things you have never done before and have no idea how to do, so you can experience the thrill of surrendering to Me and letting Me empower you to do what you could never have done on your own.

When you lie at My feet, completely surrendered and utterly dependent on Me, asking Me to do it in you, for you, through you, and even despite all your felt inadequacies ... that's when you experience the joy and miraculous wonders that come through oneness with Me. 2 Corinthians 12:9-10.

When you listen to Satan's lies and receive them as truth, he brings more negative experiences into your life to confirm those lies.

But the good news is, when I set you free, you just might find I've healed *all* the memories linked to that lie.

What did I set you free from in the Truth encounter you wrote about on pages 44-45? Ask me to show you another memory linked to that lie. Then go there with Me. How does it feel now? Can you tell the difference? If you still don't feel free yet, seek Me for another Truth Encounter for that memory. There may be other lies in there you still believe.

Whatever your struggle is, as you ask Me to set you free, ask Me also to fill you with the opposite, Kingdom Culture qualities. Instead of your anger, ask Me to fill you with grace and love. Instead of your fear, let Me fill you with peace and faith. Instead of depression, let Me give you forgiveness and hope.

My truth topples lies and sets you free. But to live in freedom, you will need to build some new habits together with Me. Over the next few days and weeks I will allow situations into your life that will bring to mind those old lies, only now, rather than feeling controlled by them, you will recognize your choice. Consciously choose My truth, ask for My help, and let Me lead you out.

If you forget to think about Me, and even if you fall, don't worry. I knew that was going to happen long before, and I already have a plan to pick you up, straighten those wobbly legs, and help you stand and run again.

The humility that comes from knowing you're not strong enough is what drives you deeper into My arms to rely on My empowering rather than your own strength.

So, ask Me to show you how the fall happened, and what led you there. There may be more lies or another memory I want to heal, or something I want to teach you that will equip you to stand strong next time. Just let Me walk with you through each situation. The more you step out in Truth and obedience, the easier it will be to hear My voice and follow My lead, until all those old thoughts and triggers disappear and your struggle with that stronghold is gone.

Once I've shown you a stronghold I want to set you free from, the enemy may thrash at you a bit in that area of your life. But don't get discouraged. Rather, take heart, because his anger is a sign that you're headed in My directions. Keep moving toward Me, letting Me teach you and tear down all those prison walls so you will be fully free.

Do you want Me to empower you to do greater things than you could ever imagine? Then throw off everything that's holding you back, and run as one with Me. Hebrews 12:1-3, John 14:12-14.

Lord, how do You see my sin? I want to hate it. I want to be so repulsed by how my sin affects others and grieves You that I never return to it again.

Ask Me for a picture of what freedom will look like. Let Me paint it on your heart and mind, so you'll keep heading that way, even when the going gets rough.

One way to let My truth trample your lies is to do a Word Search. Look up in a concordance all the verses about your issue. For example, when you struggle with fear, look up "fear," "afraid," "tremble," "anxious," but also the opposite, "peace," "faith," "trust," "love," "hope." Write down what I show you through those verses in your journal or in the margin of your Bible, so you don't forget. Then go back to it often to re-read what I said to you, until you know that truth is deep within and the lies are gone.

Let the truth you know be the truth you live.

All of My truth is in My Word, so read it, study it, memorize it, know it. Let Me point you to just what you need when you need it.

55

Do you want to know a sure way to pray the things of My heart? Pray My Word. Take those verses that resonate with what you feel Me doing, and reword them into a prayer from your heart.

You can also pray My Word for those you love. Ask Me to lead you to just the verse that person needs, and then pray it back to Me for him/her.

I am the Word. John 1:1,14.

When you get to know My Word, you get to know Me.

And when you open up your Bible, you are looking in My eyes.

Meet with Me every night, even if just for a few minutes. Keep a Bible by your bed, and at the end of the day, read until you feel Me speaking. Then fall asleep on that word. When you awaken in the morning, let Me be your first thought.

I know you get distracted sometimes, thinking about something else as you read, and missing what I want to say to you. But think of this time with Me as a secret meeting in the Secret Place with the King you've pledged your life to.

Before you read My Word, ask Me to block out distractions and speak to you. I want you to feel My loving touch, as I plant My truth deep within you and give you the instructions you need to overcome. I love you.

Try closing your eyes and asking Me to give you a picture of what you're reading. Where am I in that picture? Where are you? What am I doing? What am I saying to you? Ask Me.

When you read about Me in the gospels, try asking Me which character in each story you are most like and why. I want to talk with you, to hear your heart, and let you hear Mine.

As you awaken each morning, ... before you open your eyes, before you think of all the many things you have to do, before you worry about that difficult meeting, ... make Me your first thought. Listen to the song I bring to your mind, or what I want to tell you about this day. Hand your day to Me, and let Me take it over and empower you for everything you will face. I already know what's going to happen, and I have a pathway through it for you that will leave you in awe of Me. I want to turn every trial into a God-awesome opportunity.

Lord, here is my schedule for the day. Is there anything I'm doing You never asked me to do? Or something You want to do that I didn't leave time for? Show me.

Morning

_____
_____
_____
_____
_____
_____
_____
_____

Afternoon

_____
_____
_____
_____
_____
_____
_____
_____
_____
_____

Evening

_____
_____
_____
_____
_____
_____

Burnout happens when you're doing more than I have asked you to do,
or you're doing it in your own strength.

Let Me be the One you seek for every plan. Proverbs 3:5-7.

Don't skip a quiet time. You'll need what I tell you to make it through the day victoriously.

Talk with Me all day long. Hand Me your thoughts as soon as you have them:
"Lord, I think.... What do You think about that?" Let Me renew your mind and
conform it to Mine. Isaiah 55:6-9.

What I'm thinking about today	What do You say about that, Lord?

Don't forget to seek Me for My plans every new season. There may be something I asked you to do last season that we're finished with, and something new I want to do together with you now. Don't miss the joy of My powerful plans.

You have time for what you make time for. Don't busy yourself so much that you miss what you were created for. Luke 10:38-42.

Lord, here is my schedule for the week. Please show me anything I have planned that You have not, and anything You want to do together with me that is not in my plan yet.

Monday
_____
_____
_____
_____

Tuesday
_____
_____
_____

Wednesday
_____
_____
_____

Thursday
_____
_____
_____

Friday
_____
_____
_____

Saturday
_____
_____
_____

Sunday
_____
_____
_____

Is it hard sometimes to say no to people who expect something of you? You will run yourself ragged trying to do everything everyone wants you to.

They don't know you like I do, and they don't know what I have planned for you. So, whenever someone asks you to do something I haven't already asked you to do, just smile and answer, *"I'll pray about that and get back to you."* Galatians 1:10. Then lay that down before Me and ask Me what My will is.

Lord, teach me how to say no in a loving way when I am urged to do something You are not asking me to do. Open my eyes to see the opportunities to love others that You are placing in my path.

You are busy with many things, fighting many battles on many fronts, but only two things have I asked you to do: Love Me and love others. If you've done these two things, then you've done everything I've asked of you. Matthew 22:37-40.

How have I been unloving toward others, Lord?

Teach me to love like You do.

Disobedience puts distance between us, making it difficult for you to hear My voice, especially when I'm whispering. But each time you obey, My voice will get louder, because you just took a huge step closer to Me. James 4:8a.

When you love Me with all your heart, you'll have no problem obeying Me, for it will be all you will want to do. John 14:15, 1 John 2:5-6.

How have I not been loving toward You, Lord?

_____
_____
_____
_____
_____
_____

Is there anything You've asked me to do I haven't done yet?

_____
_____
_____
_____
_____
_____

Is there anything You've asked me not to do that I'm still doing?

_____
_____
_____
_____
_____
_____
_____
_____
_____
_____
_____
_____
_____

What are you fighting about these days? If your purpose is to win an argument or get what you want, you're fighting the wrong battle. You have a real enemy, but it's not your brother or sister. Ephesians 6:10-12.

Whenever you find yourself in a difficult situation, don't just react, escalating the conflict. Be quick to listen, slow to speak, and slow to get angry. James 1:19. Ask Me what I'm doing, and follow Me there.

Check for sin in your heart. Did you have a part in the conflict? Matthew 7:1-5. Ask Me. If so, ask that person forgiveness. 1 John 1:8-10.

Mind-reading is dangerous. Don't imagine you know what others are thinking or what evil motives they're hiding behind their actions and words. Only I know man's thoughts, and I did not die and give you My job. So, before you accuse someone, make sure you know the facts. Ask, "When you said..., did you mean...?" James 4:11-12. Lay down all your opinions and ideas about that person and that situation at My feet and ask Me for Mine. Mark 11:11-17; Proverbs 3:5-7; Isaiah 55:6-9.

Lord, is there anyone I've misjudged? Have I imagined someone meant something they didn't say?

_____
_____
_____
_____
_____
_____
_____
_____
_____

Lord, this is what I think of this person:

_____
_____
_____
_____
_____
_____
_____
_____
_____
_____
_____

But, Lord, when You look at him (her), what do You see?

_____
_____
_____
_____

Can you see what the enemy is doing in your present situation? He's causing dissension, discouraging you, wrecking your chances for success, distancing you from Me and from others, making you anxious, angry, depressed, afraid....

I came to bring you life, but he seeks to kill, steal and destroy. John 10:10. If you don't walk close to Me, asking for My viewpoint and letting Me empower you, he will steal your joy, destroy your relationships, kill your passion for me, and lead you to dark places in your mind and heart.

So, don't let him. If he's making you angry at someone, forgive. If you feel the urge to complain, give thanks to Me instead. If you're depressed, worship Me. Whatever you see Satan doing, purpose to do the opposite.

Ask Me what I'm doing, and join Me there.

No matter how many evil things you see the enemy doing, know that I am doing much, much more. And it is good. For I am Sovereign, and I'm still in control. The enemy can't do anything unless I allow it, and if I allow it, then I am doing something important in you and through you. I love you, and I'm for you.

No matter how many things I'm doing in the midst of this trial, whether you can see them or not, I am always drawing you to Myself.

So, get a head start on that. Draw near to Me now. James 4:7-8.

Sometimes there are places in your heart that are not yet healed because you have not yet forgiven entirely.

Forgiveness is a choice, not a feeling, although the feelings may come later.

Forgiveness doesn't mean that person's sin is okay. Sin is never okay.

Forgiveness means you choose to cut the strings that tie your heart to that offense, so the enemy can't yank you around by it anymore. It means letting go of the need for revenge, and releasing that person and their sin into My hands to be dealt with by Me, so you can go back to the love, peace, joy, and all the fruit of My Spirit you were created to enjoy in Me.

So, whenever anger, hurt, or some other emotion outside the fruit of My Spirit rises up in you, get alone with Me as soon as you can, and let me set you free.

Here are some steps you can do with Me to find freedom through forgiveness:

1. Before you judge others for what they did wrong, make sure the sin isn't actually your own. Did you do something to instigate that response? Are you also in some way guilty of what you're accusing them of? Are you judging or mind-reading (deciding what they're thinking or what evil motives they had)? Matthew 7:1-5, James 4:10-12. Only I know what someone is thinking. Leave the judging up to Me.

2. Whenever you feel angry or hurt, come to Me and ask Me why you feel that way. Ask Me when was the first time that feeling or response entered your heart, and let Me take you anywhere I want to take you and show you anything I want to show you. I may take you to another memory.

3. Allow yourself to remember that event and feel what you felt when it happened. Look for the lies (like, *"Everyone's against me. I have to defend myself."*)

4. Still in that memory, feeling all those things you felt, choose to forgive.
   - Say, *"I forgive you, (name), for (offense)."*
   - Lay down all your opinions and ideas about them and ask Me for Mine.
   - Pray for them and bless them. Ask for My mercy on them to set them free from the strongholds that lead them to sin.

5. If you made a vow (like, *"I'll never let anyone do that to me again!"*), break it.

6. Ask Me for My truth, *"Lord, You were there when that happened. What were You doing and saying?"*

7. Run what you feel Me saying through the Three-Fold Sieve (page 28).

8. Now forgive the offender in your current situation. Bless him. Pray for him.

9. If the offense replays in your mind, don't worry about it, no matter how many times it happens. Just remind yourself, *"I forgive ... and I bless him in Jesus' name,"* and then pray for him again. If you continually choose to forgive, and pray all the more for others' salvation and freedom when Satan attacks you, then he will lose more ground by attacking you than not, and eventually he'll leave you alone, and that old offense won't replay in your mind anymore.

Forgive and you will be forgiven. Mark 11:25.

Have you ever made a vow, like, "I'll never let someone do that to me again?"

Self-protective vows are dangerous, because I am your Protector. You don't have what it takes to do My job. And you also don't know what's up ahead or the plans I have for you. Romans 8:28. When you choose self-protection over My protection, you actually leave yourself wide open for the enemy to attack you all the more. To break those vows and surrender once again to your Shield and Protector, try praying from your heart something like this:

"Lord, forgive me for making the vow,' _____ '
I renounce and break that vow now in Your name, Jesus, and I cancel any
rights the enemy feels he has to pick on me because of it. I release myself to
live under Your protection, O Lord, for You alone are my Shield...."

I am your Armor. Let Me cover you. Completely. Ephesians 6:10-18, Romans 13:14.

Have you planned a special getaway with Me yet? A day or a half day, or even an overnight alone with your First Love, your Best Friend, your Father, your Maker, your Refuge and Strength? I miss you. And I have so much I want to do together with you. I've been waiting for you to be still and be with Me.

You come to Me for the big decisions, but sometimes you go to others first. And the smaller decisions you often make without Me. But I have so many plans for you! Come to Me first. For every decision, no matter how small. Don't worry if you can't hear My voice straight away. I'm looking at your heart. Waiting for your surrender. When you lean on Me and ask Me to guide you, I will not let you go astray. And, oh, the adventures and the miracles I have planned for you! Even today. Even in the mundane moments. I want to make every moment a God-awesome one, filled with wonder and power.

Surrender is the key to joy and peace.

If you surrender to Me, I will not let you miss My path.

Others are watching you. Let's show them together the joy of surrender, of listening to My voice and following Me in obedience. Don't just tell them to pray. Let them see you do it.

Next time someone comes to you for advice, before you tell him your experience or what you think he should do, say, *"Let's ask God what He wants to do."* Then pray together, helping him ask Me himself. Give him a time of silence so he can listen for My reply. Then ask, *"What do you feel God saying?"* Once you hear what I'm speaking to his heart, then share with him the things I've taught you that agree with that, or verses from My Word, and whatever else I lay on your heart.

I want him to come to Me first. I love him just as I love you.

Whenever you lead a Bible study, before you start, ask everyone there to personally pray and ask Me to speak to them through My Word. This moves the encounter from horizontal, "I wonder what he's going to say about God today," to vertical, "God, what do You want to say to me today?"

Your everyday moments can become God-awesome moments
when you hand them all to Me.

As you wake up in the morning, before you open your eyes, before you think of all the things you need to get done today, think My name.
Then hand your day to Me.
Ask Me to give you a special word from My heart today, something I want to show you or teach you, or a special verse.
Then watch throughout your day for Me to do that.

Ask Me how you can bless someone today. I've got some great ideas!
Is there anything on your schedule today that's not what I have planned? Or
anything I have planned you need to make room for? Ask Me.

Ask Me to surprise you today. To do something so personal, so unique, only I could do it. Then look for that all throughout the day. Write in your journal at night what I did.

All throughout your day, look for what I'm doing. Invite Me into every situation. Even while people are talking and things are happening, ask Me, *"Lord, what are You doing? I want to follow You there."*

Don't just make decisions quickly all day today because you think you know what you're doing. Ask Me. If you're not sure what I'm saying, step out onto the most loving path (Matthew 22:37-40), and say, *"Lord, it feels You're wanting me to head this way, but if this isn't what You're doing, close the door or show me some other way what You're wanting me to do."*

I want to do everything together with You. I love you.

At night, ask Me to send anything out of your room that's not of Me, to fill it with My presence and My angels, to protect your family, your things, and your dreams. If you wake up in the night, I am there with you. Don't be afraid. Talk to Me. Worship Me. Pray. Meet Me in the watches of the night. Those are special moments, with no distractions, no responsibilities, ... just you and Me. So, rest in My presence, and enjoy Me.

If you wake up in a panic, tell the enemy, *"Get out, in the name of Jesus!"* And then worship Me. My authority is in you. The demons have to flee. And they HATE it when you worship Me.

If you have a nightmare, let Me heal it for you. Go back into the parts that distressed you most, and ask Me what I say about that. What is My truth for the lie the enemy wanted to plant in you to make you afraid, discouraged, etc. I want to transform your nightmare. And heal your mind and heart.

Whenever you lie awake at night with a million thoughts running through your head, remember My Philippians 4:4-8 plan for peace:

1. Rejoice. I am near!
2. Whatever is worrying you, hand it to Me.
3. Ask for My help and thank Me for the outcome (even if you don't know what it is yet). Romans 8:28.
4. Rest in My peace, and think on Me.
5. Worship.

Worship draws Me near and sends the enemy to flight.

Trust in Me, for I am Sovereign. Even the enemy must bow to Me. So if anything happens, know that I have a plan in the midst of it, and it is good for I am Good, even if you can't see what I'm doing yet.

No matter how hurt or angry you feel, turn TO Me, not away. You can beat on My chest, if you need to. My chest is broad enough and My heart strong enough to take it and still beat with unending love for you.

When your feet are stuck in the muck of all you're going through, and your problems are all up in your face, hear Me calling, "Come up here." Climb up onto My shoulders. Let Me show you My Eagle-eye perspective. And we'll soar over this thing together.

If your train of thoughts goes off-track, as soon as you notice, hand your thoughts to Me. Even if that train wrecks, I can still pick you up and put you back on track. Let Me.

If you feel distracted during your quiet times with all the things you need to get done, just keep a notepad next to your Bible, and write that to-do list as it comes to mind. Then go back to listening to Me.

Ask Me to protect your time with Me. And you protect it too. Turn off your phone. Tell others in your house not to disturb you.

Don't let the world and all its busy distractions keep you from Me. Rather, let ME distract YOU from the world.

No man gets everything he wants in this life, unless his desire is for more of Me. Then I will most certainly satisfy him with Myself. Psalm 37:4.

Hunger for more of Me, and I will satisfy you.

What are you afraid of? Ask Me.

Then ask Me for My truth. When you know what that is, write it down, and cross out the old fear.

My Fears	Your Truth

The man who fears Me walks so close to Me he wouldn't dare step
off My path for fear of missing My blessings.

Ask Me to show you the strongholds in your life. How did pride lead to those? How do they connect to each other? Ask Me to show you. You can draw arrows and write notes, if you like. As I set you free, mark out those strongholds.

PRIDE

Whether you think highly or lowly of yourself, it's still pride if your eyes are on you. Don't focus on your abilities or inabilities, but on My greatness.

If you need to look at yourself, then ask Me first, *"Lord, how do You see me?"* Only when you see yourself through My eyes will you see clearly.

I hate pride, because it sets self up as an idol before Me, In fact, I must tear pride down. But humility draws Me near.

Humility lays down all your thoughts and opinions and asks for Mine.

To agree with Me — that is humility.

Humility is remembering you're always in the presence of Someone greater.

Humility is total surrender to Me.

Humility is depending on Me for everything all the time.

Pride is at the heart of every argument. Make sure it's not yours..

The heart of the matter in an argument is not, "He's not listening!" or "She's so mean to me!" It's what you're focusing on that bothers you so. You can't change that other person. Only I can do that. But if you lay down your need to be right or to be heard, and ask Me what I'm doing, I just might use you to work a miracle in that situation.

You have a real enemy, but it's not your brother. Fight for him, not against him. Listen to him, have grace for him, pray for his freedom, and love him into My arms.

When you feel your emotions rising, don't just react. Excuse yourself from the situation as soon as you can, and come get alone with Me.

Lord, why do I feel this way? Where does this reaction come from? When did it first enter my life?

_____

_____

_____

_____

_____

_____

Help me feel what I felt when that happened. What were the lies I received?

_____

_____

_____

_____

_____

_____

Lord, You were there when that happened. Where were You? What were You doing? What were You saying? Show me. What is Your truth You want to speak to my heart to set me free?

_____

_____

_____

_____

_____

_____

_____

Don't shift the blame. The best way to miss what I'm showing you is to point a finger at someone else.

Be quick to listen, slow to speak and slow to get angry. James 1:19. Try answering, *"So, I hear you saying..... Is that right?"* This helps clear up misunderstanding and lowers tension so the other person feels heard.

When you feel tension rising, when things start going wrong, or something strange that makes you feel uneasy begins happening, try saying,

"If this is the enemy, in the name of Jesus, stop it!"

If others are upset at you, ask Me to help you remain silent, and then when they calm down a little, set up an appointment to talk about the subject later. Pray ahead of time, asking Me to cover that time together, and then start the meeting with prayer, inviting Me to guide both of you in everything you think and say.

Don't just receive what others say to you or about you. Hand criticism or a message others claim is "from God" back over to Me. Let Me show you what is true and what is not. Hurt people hurt people, and even when I am the One speaking to them, they may filter My words through their strongholds and twist them. Use My Three Fold Sieve to make sure what others say or what you receive is from Me. (page 28).

The best way to lead others in right paths is to walk that way yourself. Let Me change you first, then you'll see a change in those around you.

Most of the problems you have with others can be resolved within yourself by letting Me heal you. But sometimes, if someone's sin habit is hurting My body, I may ask you to talk with him/her about it. In that case, let Matthew 18:15-17 be your guide:

1. Don't talk behind his back. If you have a problem with him, go to him personally.

2. Make sure what you're confronting him on is sin, not just something you don't like about him or disagree with.

3. Speak the truth in love.

   1) Clean your own heart out first.

   2) Make sure no judgment clouds your view. Matthew 7:1-5.

   3) Lay down all your opinions about him, and ask Me for Mine.

   4) Set up a time to meet with him, and start that meeting with prayer, asking Me to guide your thoughts and words.

   5) Speak the truth in love. Ephesians 4:15. Let Me give you scriptures I can encourage him through. Ask questions that will help him share his heart, so you can listen well. Pray for him. Matthew 18:18-20.

4. If he listens, then you have your brother back. But if he doesn't, go and find others he respects, a friend who also has been affected by the situation, a counselor, a leader, or someone else I send you to, and meet with him again together with that person(s).

When others (or even you) say negative things about you, come to Me. Let's cut off those curses together and draw you into My protection. You can pray something like this, and anything else I lead you to do or say:

"In the name of Jesus, I cut off from myself the words, "_____
_____" and any
negative effects or curses that may have fallen upon me or my children because
of them. I break that curse and any others in the name of Jesus, and declare
that I belong to God and I am who He says I am. I am _____
_____ (Kingdom Culture opposite
what that curse said). In the name of Jesus, I forbid the enemy to pick on me,
my children, or my children's children ever again with regard to that now-broken
curse, and I release God's _____
_____ (Kingdom Culture qualities that are opposite
what the enemy says about me, like the fruit of the Spirit) over me, my children,
and their children for all generations, in the name of Jesus...."

Have you spoken when you should have been silent? Have you said something you've regretted? Hurt someone? Slandered them? Talked behind their back? Assumed something about them that wasn't true and then accused them, or told others? Ask Me to put a guard on your mouth and use your tongue to love, to bless, and to bring Me glory. And if there's anyone you need to ask forgiveness from, for using your tongue as a weapon against them, do that. I'll help you. We can do it together.

Your words have power. So use them to open up channels of blessings to flow through them from Me to you and to the people around you.

Seek an eternal mindset, My son. Whenever you're impatient because you have to wait in line, pray for each of those people, or ask Me to help you start a conversation with someone so you can share My love. When appliances break, use it as a chance to show love to the repairman. When others are angry at you, ask Me to show you what's going on in their lives, so you can pray for them and love them, and let Me use you to draw them back to Me. Love is eternal. Love Me and love others. Then you've done everything I've asked you to do. Matthew 22:37-40.

One great way to go on the offensive against the enemy is to use his attacks as a prayer prompt for eternal things. Pray for the salvation of lost people you know, or for an unreached people group. Pray for freedom from strongholds for those who are struggling. Pray for My heaven to open up and pour down miracles and blessings to surprise the people around you and draw them to Me. If you pray more for eternal things when the enemy attacks you with sickness, worry, stress, fear, or other earthly issues, he will eventually quit, because he loses more ground attacking you than not.

Whenever you feel frustrated, take a step back to look and see what expectations you had that didn't get met. People and circumstances will fail you, but I never fail. I may not do what you want Me to when you want Me to, but expect Me, because *I'm always happening*. Look for what I'm doing and join Me there.

Seek My instructions every day and through every trial. I have a way through this. If you ride on My pinions, you'll feel My joy, even in the midst of difficulty.

Don't just receive what others say about you, especially if it's negative. Hand it back to Me and let Me show you what's true and what's not. And definitely don't listen to the enemy's lies about you. Ask Me, *"Lord, when You look at me, what do You see?"* Only when you see through My eyes will you understand fully who you are and all I created you to be.

Love those who persecute you and you will triumph over the enemy.
Romans 12:14-21.

Don't fight against people, but *for* them. Fight for their freedom. For greater oneness with each other and with Me. For truth, humility and righteousness. Fight on the winning side. Psalm 45:3-7.

I ask you to treat older men and women as your fathers and mothers, and younger men and women as your brothers and sisters in all purity. 1 Timothy 5:1-2.

Whenever My temple (your body, heart, and wife, there is a tie that binds you to that person in ways only meant for holy matrimony. 1 Corinthians 6:12-20, Genesis 2:24, Matthew 5:28.

Through that thought or event, whether you were a victim or a willing participant, a door is opened for the enemy to assault you all the more with sexual thoughts, sins, temptations, dreams, or abuse.

But we can overcome this together, My beloved son. I want to set you free. To cleanse you, heal you, make you like new again. Will you let Me?

First, repent of your involvement, and seek Me for a Truth Encounter (page 44), so we can find the lies that lead you back there, and knock them down with My truth. Ask Me to be a Shield around your mind, heart, and body, to guard all your intimate thoughts, caresses, and kisses. Let Me help you build wide hedges around the situations that tempt you so you won't walk into a trap.

And, together, let's cut off whatever rights the enemy feels he has to pick on you. To break soul ties to the person(s) involved, pray something like this:

"Lord forgive me for _____. In the name of Jesus, I break any unholy ties to _____ (person's name), and I bless her (him) and her (his) marriage, and my own as well, to be founded on You, for You alone are True Love. If anything unholy has passed to me from her (him) or from me to her (him), I cut that off now in Your name, Jesus, and I release myself to be Yours, for You are True Love, and my body is Your temple. I ask You to redeem whatever was lost in that unholy union. Set me free from the thought processes that lead me in wrong directions, and set me apart for the one You have chosen for me to marry. Teach me how to remain pure and led by Your Spirit in all my choices and thoughts. Help me be the man of God you created me to be as a brother to my sisters and brothers, and as a husband to my wife. Lead me in Your right paths, empowered by Your Spirit. I want to be one with You, Lord, for I am Yours and You are mine...."

Whatever you hold in secret the enemy can use against you. Give Me your secrets. Talk to Me. Let Me release you from those secret sins and set you free. Ask Me to lead you to someone trustworthy who loves Me and whom you can talk with about that, so he can pray for you and help keep you accountable, as you seek to walk out in new obedience to Me.

Is there anything you haven't given me yet? What's holding you back? Lay it down.

My concern is not so much that you are happy doing what you want in life, but that you truly know Me. For happiness is fleeting. But the joy that comes from obedience is eternal. Delight in Me and I will satisfy your longing with Myself.
Psalm 37:4.

My love, I want to be in every area of your life. For I have plans for each encounter, task and relationship. But if you do not invite Me into that encounter,
you may miss what I am doing. And that is something you won't want to miss!
Jeremiah 29:11.

Invite Me into your day today. Ask Me what I am doing and follow Me there. Do you already have a full to-do list? Ask Me what I want you to cross out or add. Don't worry if you feel you can't hear My voice. Just surrender your schedule to Me, and trust Me to lead you. Proverbs 3:5-6.

I speak in many ways. So, if you're expecting Me to say what you want or to say it in a certain way, you may miss My voice. Just open your heart to Me. Ask Me to speak to you any way I desire. Then look for My answer throughout the day. I'm with you. I'm not hiding to make you feel you can't find Me. I'm drawing you in closer. For if you want to hear My whisper, you must draw near. James 4:8a.

Power comes through surrender. If you want Me to empower you for every situation you're in right now, then lay all your agendas down at My feet and ask Me for Mine.

I know what is best for you better than you know yourself. For only I can see what is around the next corner or what you will face many years from now.
Just trust Me. Take My hand and let Me lead you.
Don't hold back or you will miss the treasures I have for you all along the way.

A man of power is a man of worship. Worship Me, for I am worthy.

Is there a gift you've longed for? Ask Me for it. For every good gift and every perfect gift comes from Me. Matthew 7:11.

Have I not told you that anything you ask for in My name I will do? Believe. And walk as one with Me. When your desires are My desires, you can ask whatever you desire and it will be done for you. John 15:7.

If you desire wisdom, then ask Me for it. I Myself am Wisdom, and I live within you. So the Wisdom you seek is not so far away. 1 Corinthians 1:26-30.

Seek Me and you will find Me, if you look for Me in earnest. Jeremiah 29:13-14.

I speak in many ways, but whatever I say to you will always agree with My character of love and grace, and My Word—not just one portion of it, but all of it.

My Word is best interpreted by My Word. So, if you are taking a stand that doesn't agree with the rest of Scripture, then there's something wrong with your interpretation of that passage, not My Word. Lay down all your human reasoning and wrap your heart and mind around Me as God. I am not limited to human explanations, expectations, or reasoning. I am God Almighty. I am that I am. Run your beliefs through My Three-Fold Sieve (page 28), and make sure they hold strong before you teach them or judge someone by them.

When you don't know, ... when you don't understand, ... when things aren't what you thought they were, ... just trust Me. I'm still in control and I know what I'm doing.

Be still. For you do not yet know how this matter will turn out. Ruth 3:18.

One way I speak to you is through urgings. Look for My Spirit nudging you throughout the day to speak to someone, to help, to do something unexpected, to bless, to encourage, to talk with Me. I'm with you and I want to empower you. Remember, anything I ask you to do will agree with My Word and with My character, especially My love. 1 John 4:16.

You don't have to do this on your own. I want to empower you.
To do it with you. Through you. FOR you.

If you love Me, you will obey My commands. In fact, that is all you will want to do! For My commands are not burdensome, but bring life to your soul and joy to your step. In obeying Me you are complete. John 14:15, Psalm 119:14.

Anything I say to you or ask you to do will draw you and others closer to Myself. Remember our Three-Fold Sieve. Does it agree with My Word? With My character of love? Does it draw you closer to Me? Then step out in confidence, My son, for I am leading you there.

You don't yet know the battles you will face today. But I know. And I'm waiting for you there in the midst of them. So, ask Me to arm you with a Scripture you will need today, from My heart to yours, to make you more than a conqueror in this fight.

Put on all your armor. Leave no part exposed. Ephesians 6:10-18.

It is not in your own power that you stand. But in Me. Let Me empower you.
Philippians 4:13.

Don't keep looking at how big your trial is. Remember how big your God is. With Me, nothing is impossible. Matthew 19:26.

Buckle up with the belt of Truth. I will keep you safe from the lies the enemy is throwing at you. John 8:31-32; 14:15-17.

What truth have I told you that you're not believing? That you can do all things through My strength? That you don't have to work yourself to the bone in order for Me to love you and see you as worthy?

Ask Me to show you in My Word all the places where I say that. Use a concordance, if you like, to look up a word or phrase you're struggling with.

Grab hold of My truth and LIVE it.

Ask Me if there's someone I would like to mentor you to grow deeper in your faith, someone who will pray for you and be an accountability partner to help you in the areas where you're struggling. I created My body to be one together, to help each other listen to Me and follow My lead.

Is there someone I want you to mentor to help him walk in greater oneness with Me? Ask Me.

When you gave your heart to Me, I became your Lord. You don't belong to the enemy. You don't have to bend to his purposes ever again.

But if you or someone in your family has been involved in occult activity, even if it was several generations ago or before you became a Christian, a door was opened to the enemy that may need to be closed now. Let's do it together:

Lord, please forgive me and others in my family for any way we have opened a door to the enemy and allowed him to speak to us. On behalf of my forefathers I repent of and renounce any occult activity, and I close the door on the enemy. I forbid him to pick on me or my children or my children's children ever again, and I break any curse that has fallen on us because of those activities or any vows made to Satan and his causes. I send the spirit of death, and any other evil spirits who feel they have a right to pick on me and my family, to the feet of Jesus to be dealt with by Him. And I forbid you, in Jesus' name, ever to return. I declare life over me and my family and the generations yet to come, in the name of Jesus. I ask You, Lord, to wash us in Your cleansing blood, and be a Shield around us, so that anytime the enemy tries to get to us, he will have to go through You. Please protect us from any enemy schemes and bring forth only Your purposes in our lives. Fill us with all the fullness of Your love, joy, and peace, and mature us in You to attain the whole measure of the fullness of Christ. May I and my family give You glory all the days of our lives... In Your name. Amen.

Whatever strongholds I free you from or doors to the enemy I show you to shut, keep looking to Me for more instructions. I may have some more things I want you to walk through in order to be fully free.

Do you have any souvenirs or objects in your house that were used for worship to other "gods"? Ask Me to show you, and then ask Me how I want you to destroy or get rid of them. Pray through each of the rooms of your house, and dedicate your entire home to Me. Ask Me to send out anything that is not of Me and to fill your home with My presence and My angels.

Any time you travel and stay in a hotel room "clean" it out spiritually (see above), and ask Me to protect your dreams. Clean out your own home periodically, as well. Make it a safe place so full of Me there's no room for the enemy, and anyone who walks into your home will walk into My felt presence.

Have others been holding you back from doing the things I've called you to? Ask Me for My instructions through this trial. Trust Me to open the way for you, and be ready to walk that path when I open it.

Worship brings Me near and breaks the power of the enemy. So, as you worship Me, intercede for the things of My heart, for freedom for the captives, for nations and peoples, and even your neighbors and family members who still do not know Me. Let's break the chains together.

Be still and know I am God.
I love you, and I am fighting for you. Exodus 14:14.

Deepen your oneness with Christ through these Bible studies, journals, and other books from inspirational author
Mikaela Vincent

More Than A Conqueror Books.com

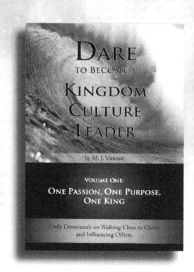 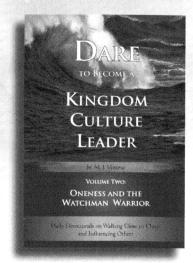

Dare to Become a Kingdom Culture Leader
Volume One: One Passion, One Purpose, One King
Volume Two: Oneness and the Watchman Warrior

Step into the destiny you were created for.
Become a Kingdom Culture Leader.

Whether you're a parent, teacher, pastor, missionary, worship leader, or even just Joe Blow Christian, this Bible study workbook to write in is for you. Through practical lessons on listening to God's voice, making wise decisions, following the Spirit's leading, walking in humility, promoting unity, and leading others well, author Mikaela Vincent uses small group Bible studies that can also be studied as a daily devotional to dig deep into the Bible and form new thought processes and habits so we can walk as one with Christ and lead out as Kingdom Culture influencers.

Dare to Become a Kingdom Culture Leader is based on the New Testament model of the church as the body of Christ, with the Lord as the Head, and offers steps for experiencing God, spiritual warfare, and following Jesus' calling in parenting, pastoring, mentoring and other leadership roles.

Dare to Be a Man of God

Powerful Bible studies for young men today on listening to God's voice and winning life's battles

Pull out your "sword" and get ready for a dive into the Word that just might change your life! This workbook for single men offers practical tools for knowing God's voice, overcoming strongholds, tapping into the Spirit's power, finding the wife your King has chosen for you, and pushing back the darkness. Step into the adventure today, and dare to be a true man of God! A leader's guide is included, but the studies can also be done as private devotionals. We recommend this workbook for any single man 14 years and older. (For younger ages, try *Dare to Become a Man of God*).

Dare to Be a Man of God Prayer Journal

Take this companion to *Dare to Be a Man of God* into your quiet times for some exciting conversations with the King. Packed full with tools for recognizing God's voice and walking as one with Him, this notebook to write in is available with or without lines.

Dare to Become a Man of God

30 Bible studies from a mother's heart to her son's on drawing near to Christ and living victoriously.

Whether you like it or not, you are at war. Will you dare to defy enemy schemes? Will you dare to fight for the things that matter? Will you dare to become a man of God? Cartoons, personal stories, deep questions, practical how-to steps, and Scripture all point youth ages 12 and up to fix their eyes on Jesus and draw near to Him as they fight the good fight, listen to God's voice and make wise decisions through His guidance, so they can become more than conquerors through every tough situation life presents. A leader's guide is included, but this workbook can also be studied as a devotional in personal quiet times.

Delight to Be a Woman of God

Deep Bible studies for Christian single women today on listening to God's voice, walking in the Spirit, unlocking your beauty, and finding true love, happiness and freedom

Do you long for true love? Are you tired of falling into the same old messes again and again? Do you desire to be truly beautiful? Packed full with tools for hearing God's voice, finding freedom from strongholds and lies, and walking in the Spirit's power, this Bible study guide by Mikaela Vincent will strengthen your faith, transform your mind, and empower you to overcome. A leader's guide is included, but this workbook can also be used for personal devotionals. Recommended for ages 14 and above. For younger women, try *Delight to Become a Woman of God*.

Delight to Be a Woman of God Prayer Journal

This companion to *Delight to Be a Woman of God* is full of tools for recognizing God's voice and walking as one with Him. Available with or without lines.

Delight to Become a Woman of God

30 Bible studies from a mother's heart to her daughter's on drawing near to Christ and loving well

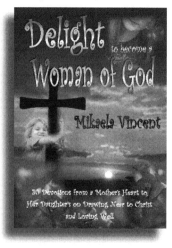

It's not a fairy tale. It's true. You really are a princess, destined to marry the King. And together you'll live happily forever after. It's all you ever dreamed life could be, and it's all yours, if you choose to become a woman of God. This Bible study guide for young women ages 12 and above, offers original illustrations, personal stories, deep questions, and Scripture to point young women to deeper depths with Christ so they can be set free from the things that keep them from the abundant life they were created for. A group study leader's guide is included. But this workbook can also be used for personal quiet times.

Pure-As-Gold Children's Books
by Mikaela Vincent
www.MoreThanAConquerorBooks.com
Equipping young hearts today for the battles of tomorrow.

Out You Go, Fear!

Is your child afraid of the night? Does he sometimes "see" monsters in the dark? Does she have nightmares or awake in a panic? Do you? This story about a fearful, but eventually brave boy addresses night fears most children experience. Through colorful pictures, sound truths, and a fun storyline, Vincent offers children ages 4-8 (and parents too!) steps to freedom from fear so they can sleep in peace. Includes tips for parents on helping their children to freedom from nightmares and the effects of traumatic memories.

I Want a Horse

Have you ever wanted something so much it was all you could think of or dream about? In this inspirational picture book for ages 4-8, Mikaela Vincent uses colorful artwork, imaginative poetry and heartwarming humor to tell the story of a young girl who asks for her heart's desire only to discover a treasure she already has that surpasses her imaginations. Moms and daughters will especially enjoy a deep bond reading together this fun interchange between an ambitious little girl and her wise and creative mother.

I Want to See Jesus

This easy-to-read book for ages 3-7 uses colorful drawings and simple words to teach just-beginning readers that Jesus is always with us, even when we can't see Him.

Chronicles of the Kingdom of Light
fantasy with purpose
by Mikaela Vincent

Based on stories created by Mikaela Vincent to help her children live who they are in Christ, some have compared these first two books in the *Chronicles of the Kingdom of Light* to the *Chronicles of Narnia* because of the inspirational allegory filled with adventure, humor, illustrations, and truths that just might change your life, including freedom from fear, lies, and strongholds.

Book 1: Rescue from Darkness

Book 2: Sands of Surrender

Snatched from their summer fun by a sudden tragedy, six friends loyal to the King of Light embark upon an unforgettable adventure into the Kingdom of Darkness to rescue a young boy held hostage by evil creatures.

Astride such mystical mounts as a winged tiger, a flying unicorn, and a giant cobra, these ordinary young people engage in an extraordinary battle that will cost them more than they counted on. As they struggle against monsters — and even each other — to overcome the fight against night, the friends soon discover the true enemy that must be conquered is the enemy within themselves.

Banished by the King of Light, Cory cannot continue the search for his kidnapped brother until he discovers a way back into the Kingdom of Darkness where the boy is held prisoner.

When creatures of Darkness offer to lead him there, his decision to follow costs him his freedom and exposes a plot against his family so dangerous he may not make it out alive.

Meanwhile, Victoria sets out on her own misadventure to rescue her friend, but her decisions place those she loves in such terrible peril, Cory's life is not the only one she must save.

Follow, friend, like Mikaela Vincent, and share with others:

Facebook Page: **Mikaela.Vincent.author**
Facebook Profile: **Mikaela.Vincent.MoreThanAConquerorBooks**
Instagram: **Mikaela.Vincent**
Twitter: **Mikaela_Vincent**
Pinterest: **Mikaela Vincent: More Than A Conqueror Books**
Blog: **www.MoreThanAConquerorBooks.wordpress.com**

Mikaela Vincent serves God with her husband in a dark area of the world where few have ever heard the name of Jesus. All her books were written together with the Lord in their quiet times to influence her children and those she mentors to become all God created them to be —

more than conquerors.

All proceeds received by the author go to shining Light in the darkness. If you'd like to know more about how you can help Mikaela and her ministry, or if you have any questions, write MoreThanAConquerorBooks@gmail.com.

Thank you for being a part of catching the world on fire for the One Who created it for His glory.

Step into the adventure...

Mikaela Vincent
More Than A Conqueror Books

We're not just about books. We're about books that make a difference in the lives of those you care about.

www.MoreThanAConquerorBooks.com

83404765R00100

Made in the USA
Columbia, SC
10 December 2017